D1432917

THE SATIRES OF
HORACE

translated by William Matthews

CPL
AUSABLE PRESS
2002

Cover art: Piero della Francesca, *Exaltation of the Cross* (detail)

Design and composition by Ausable Press.
The types faces are Poliphilus, Blado, and Charlemagne.
Cover design by Rebecca Soderholm.

Published by:
AUSABLE PRESS
46 East Hill Road, Keene NY 12942
www.ausablepress.com

ACKNOWLEDGEMENTS:
Colorado Review: I, ii; *Ohio Review:* I, ix; *Marlboro Review:* II, v;
Pequod: I, vii; *Poetry:* I, i; I, iii; *Poetry Miscellany:* I, viii

LIBRARY OF CONGRESS CATALOGING-IN-PUBLICATION DATA
Horace.
   [Satirae. English.]
   The satires of Horace / translated by William Matthews.
     p. cm.
   ISBN 1-931337-00-4 (alk. paper)—ISBN 1-931337-01-2 (pbk.
   : alk paper)
   1. Verse satire, Latin—Translations into English. 2. Rome—Poetry.
I. Matthews, William, 1942- II. Title.
   PA6396.S3 M38 2002
871'.01—dc21
                                2002066528

ALSO BY WILLIAM MATTHEWS:

THE SATIRES OF HORACE

I, i.

WHY IS IT, Maecenas, that no man's pleased
with his lot, be it chosen or thrust upon him,
but loudly praises the paths trudged on by others?
"Oh fortunate traders," cries the soldier,
his body creaking from years of hard duty.
Yet when south winds toss his ships about, the trader
cries, "A soldier's life is better. Why? Lines get drawn;
men clash; then there's swift death or joyful victory."
The lawyer or urban hotshot, when at dawn
a client pounds on his door, seeking advice, praises
the farmer. But the farmer, hauled into town
by subpoena, sings out that only urban folks
are happy. Tales like this, and there are many,
could silence that motormouth, Fabius. I'll be brief;
here's what I think. If an opportune god
were to say, "Listen up. Your wishes are granted.
You soldiers are traders; you lawyers are farmers.
Switch places and be gone. Well, why are you still here?"
They'd refuse. And yet they could be happy.
Why shouldn't Jove puff out his angry cheeks
at them and threaten not to waste his time
again listening to their fickle prayers?
I've no urge to skitter past my point, winking
like a professional wit—though what bars us
from telling truths with a laugh, the way teachers

sow cookies and reap memorized alphabets?—
but all jokes aside, what about human longings?
The farmer who blunts his plow in heavy loam,
the crooked innkeeper, the bone-rusted soldier,
the sea-scouring sailors, they all protest they'd
have quit long ago except they've got an old age
to mount sandbags against, no trickle but a flood.
Their model is the small, diligent ant, dragging
with her jaws what she can and heaving it onto
the heap she's been making because there's a next day
and one after that. Yet as soon as Aquarius signals
the year's been upended, the ant scurries no more
but stays home to live on what she's wisely gathered.
But you? Neither fierce heat nor winter, fire, sea,
nor sword can deflect you from accumulation.
Nothing will stop you till no man else be richer.
What good is your tonnage of silver and gold
if fear drives you to bury it stealthily?
"But if I use it, I'd soon be down to a penny."
But if you don't use it, what is its beauty?
If you've got a hundred thousand bushels
of grain on your threshing room floor does
your belly then hold more than mine? Suppose
you were the slave who shouldered the bread-bag,
would you eat more than he who carried none?
Tell me this, what difference does it make
to a man with a sense of proportion
if he ploughs a hundred acres or a thousand?
If I can take just as much from my grain-bins,

what's the advantage of your granaries?
Suppose you wanted a drink, no more than a jug
or a cup, and said "I'd rather drink it
from a wide river than from this puny brook?"
What then if the river rise, as if to match
your greed? The fierce Aufidus would swirl you
downstream along with its undermined banks.
The man who slakes only his thirst won't drink mud
with his water, and won't drown. But most people
want all that they desire, and so say, "There's no such
thing as too much: you are what you acquire."
You can always tell such a man but you
can't tell him much. Tell him to suffer, since
that's his choice. He's like the miser in Athens
who scorned, it's said, what people thought of him.
"They hiss me in the streets, but once I'm home
I stare at my bright coffers and applaud
myself." Parched Tantalus gapes with cracked lips
at receding waters...you laugh? Change but
the names and this old story's about you.
You sleep open-mouthed on a mound of money
bags but won't touch them; you just stare at them
as if they were a collection of paintings.
What's money for? What can it do? Why not
buy bread, vegetables, what you think's wine enough?
Don't you want what it harms us not to have?
Instead you lie awake in bed half-dead and stiff
as a plank from fear of broad-daylight thieves,
dead-of-night thieves, fire, vengeful and fleeing slaves—

is this the bounty you foreswore pleasure for?
If so, let me be poorest of the poor.
    "But what if chills seep through your body,
and pain beats on you like a woodpecker
and you're pinned to your bed, who will bring you
balms and sit with you and call the doc and send
you home whole to your family?" Your wife?
Your son? They have a common enemy. Pals,
neighbors, kids? When you loved money more
than them, they kept, as you did, accounts.
You didn't get your relatives by speculation.
But if you tried to call on their love now,
it would be like trying to train a mule
as a racehorse.
                    In short, set some target
for your avarice, and as your gains increase,
lessen your fear of poverty a similar amount,
and when you have reached your goal, stop
slaving for more, lest you wind up like
fabled Ummidius. His story isn't long:
he was so rich he weighed his money,
so stingy he dressed no better than a slave,
and he feared he would die of starvation
until his last hour, when a freedwoman,
a regular Clytemnestra, halved him with an axe.
    "What would you have me do then, live like
Naevius or Nomentanus, both spendthrifts?"
Don't veer from one opposite to the other
in your argument or your life: be neither

a miser nor a flashy prodigal. There's some
mean between a eunuch and a Priapus.
Things have their just proportions. So find them,
then shun too little and too much alike.

Now I'm back where I began, noticing how
no greedy man can be content, but praises
the lot of others, sulks because his neighbor's
goat's got a more bloated udder, and compares
himself not to the majority of men
but to the rich and famous. In that race
you're always breathing dust. The chariots
burst from the starting gate, and each driver
strives after those ahead of him, who pay him
no heed, nor does he think of those who chase
the clatter and clods of dirt his horses cause.
No wonder it's rare that one of them will claim
a happy life or, when that life's sped past him,
resign like a thankful guest who's eaten well.

Enough wisdom. I'll prattle on but one more line,
lest you mistake me for Crispinus, that verbose prig.

I, ii.

STRIPPERS, peddlars of elixirs, beggars,
actresses, comics—the whole tribe laments
the death of Tigellius, the singer.
"He was so generous." But another man
won't help a friend fend off cold or hunger
lest people see him as an easy mark.
And another, if you should ask him
why he's ransacked a fine inheritance
to stuff his thankless gut; buying any
gourmet tidbit he can find with borrowed
money, will tell you he'd not like to be
called stingy. Some praise and some condemn him.
Fufidius fears a reputation
as a wastrel, though he's got land galore,
though he's a master loan shark (he takes five
per cent a month, not one, and he takes all
his interest off the loan at the start),
and the more his debtor staggers under
his payments, the harder Fufidius
rides him. He likes to make loans to young men
who've just donned the toga, with strict fathers.
"Good lord," everyone says who knows of him,
"he must live like a king on all of that."
But no, he's as hard on himself as that

man in Terence's play who banishes
his son and then berates himself for life.

　"So what's the point?" you want to know. In flight
from one vice, fools crash into its opposite.
Maltinus lets his robes trail on the street;
somebody else, a real clothes horse, wears his
so snug to his crotch it's embarrassing.
Rufillus smells like a perfume stall,
and Gargonius like a goat. Is there
no middle path? Some men like only women
who drape themselves from throat to ankle just
as modest married women dress, and yet
others want only women on display
in the worst whorehouses. Seeing a man
he knew come out of such a place, Cato
(who else would have done this?) praised him: "Keep up
the good work, lad. When lust dilates your wand,
it's better to come down here than to grind
against other men's wives." "I'd not be praised
on that account," says Cupiennius,
who likes a pink and well-washed wifely cunt.

　Do you like tales in which adulterers
are scourged and set upon, in which they rent
each spasm at great cost and huge peril?
Lend me, then, your ears. One man hurled himself
from a roof. Another got flogged to death.
A third fled from a sweaty bed into
a band of savage thieves. Another
had to buy back his life. A fifth got gang-

banged by stable-boys. Another bedroom
free lance got himself deballed and delanced.
"Perfectly legal," everyone ruled—
with Judge Galba, who's lifted more nighties
than caseloads, dissenting.

                      Nor is it safe
to chase not wives but unmarried
freedwomen. Sallust hunts them as hotly
as one who beds others' wives. Does he show
good sense and the sort of generosity
manners and economics, combined, would
suggest? Not at all. He festoons his tarts
with bankrupting gifts. And, worse, he acts like
an ethical marvel. Why? "I don't stalk
married women." Does that fatuous boast
remind you of Marsaeus, who gave his
lover, Origo, his ancestral
fortune and his land: "I'll never meddle
with other men's wives." Though whores are fair game,
and actresses, they'll drain your good name
faster than your estate. OK, you're not
an adulterer, you're a pushover.
Your reputation in tatters, and your
estate depleted: this is disaster
no matter if you choose a giggling wench
for your accomplice, or some secretly
sultry matron.

                  Vilius came to see
Fausta so often that snide gossips joked

he was her father's son-in-law. Perhaps
her noble name attracted him. It had
attracted her a husband and some
other lovers, too, so when Vilius
came by one day he got himself beat up,
threatened at swordpoint, also locked out
while Longarenus sweated happily
inside. Suppose a man enduring such
disgrace had also to be scolded by
his cock: "What's wrong with you? When I'm just up
to my old tricks, do I ask you for cunt
swaddled in velvet, a consul's daughter's?"
How might he plead? "She's got a great pedigree?"
Nature offers a plan the opposite of
yours, and a panoply of pleasures, too.
You'll need to be smarter—not to confuse
what you might like with what might damage you.
Is it fate's fault, or yours, that you're in pain?
Don't sulk. Stop chasing wives. Hasn't such sport
been not the rapture you hoped for but shame
and flubs you might have spared yourself? I know
who won't agree with me (you, Cerinthus),
but neither emeralds nor pearls can make
a matron's thigh lovelier than a slut's.
Who shows and who conceals her wares? Who walks
and who puts her best foot forward? At horse
auctions the rich (who else attends?) like
to have the merchandise draped, for often
a shapely horse has tender feet, and thus

the buyer's not distracted by a small
head, a regal neck, or lovely haunches.
You might imitate their wisdom, and not
focus, like keen-eyed Lynceus, only
on a body's highlights, but gaze blindly
as Hypsaea on its flaws. "Those legs! Those arms!"
you swoon, but she's also got bony hips,
a long nose, boat-sized feet and a duck's butt.
Wives' faces you can judge; a wifely
dress conceals the rest; unless you find one
as brazen as Catia. Of course some men
don't think a campaign counts that won't exact
long siege, and if you're one of those, watch out.
Attendants, litter-bearers, hairdressers,
a swarmy entourage, an ankle-length gown—
all these will block you from a look at her.
But if you pick the right kind of woman, no
problem. She'll wear but gauzy silk you can
see through, and you can take your time to take
her measure. Do her legs please you? Her feet?
Or would you rather unwrap her
and learn what you've bought? "A hunter trails
a hare through drifted snow, but when she rests,
then so does he," the poet wrote, and next:
"My love's like that: I spurn what I could have
and chase what I can't catch." Can lines like these
console, distract or mend the broken heart
they diagnose so cannily? You might instead
wonder if unopposed desire is part

of nature's plan, and if she doesn't poise
her fallow times against her burgeonings
for her survival's sake. Suppose you're parched?
Would you insist on a gold goblet? Or
you're hungry? You'll eat nothing but pheasant
or turbot? And what if your cock should rise
to its own occasion, and a serving-
girl or -boy were near enough to serve you,
would you be too stiff to be helped? Not I.
A bard in the bush is worth two in the hand.
I hate to hear "Later" and "What I need"
and "When my husband is gone," but I like
to hear "Sure" and small talk of small money
and "Now." She who says these fine things should be
pretty and clean and offer herself as she
is, no make-up, no heels. When her left thigh
is underneath my right, I might call her
Contessa, or Milady, whatever
I like. Nor do I fear that while we fuck
her husband will come home early, the door
crash open, the dog bark, the house fill up
with furor and commotion; nor that she,
pale as her sheets, will bolt from bed, and her
accomplice, her maid, will cry out, cringing,
already fearing a beating, just as
the wife fears for her dowry and I for
my hide. Barefoot, tunic flapping, I flee
to save my ass, my money and my name.
It's hell to be caught; just ask Fabius.

I,iii.

ALL SINGERS have this fault: if friends ask them
to sing, they're shy; if they're unasked, they won't
shut up. Tigellius, the Sardinian
nightingale, was like that. Octavian
could force him to sing, of course, but should he
ask as a friend, or as his father's friend,
Tigellius's beak would be sealed. But when
the mood was on him, he'd belt out "Hello
Bacchus" all through dinner—in falsetto,
maybe, and then, a dish-rattling basso.
Consistent? He was a great bunch of guys.
Sometimes he'd run as if from enemies.
More often he'd glide slowly, like a girl
in a religious procession. One day
he'd own two hundred slaves. The next day? Ten.
Thursday he'd prattle dreamily of kings.
On Friday he'd rail against pomp: "I need but
a table that won't wobble, salt, and clothes
enough to warm my body." Well then, give
this undemanding soul a million
sesterces, and in five days they'd be gone.
He seldom slept till dawn, and then he'd furl
up like a cat and sleep all day. He took

the prize for being out of step.
                              "Well then,"
someone might berate me, "have you no flaws?"
Some, but not those. Mine may be lesser ones.
Once Maenius was bitching about
Novius, behind his back, of course, and so
someone said to him, "Look here, what about
yourself? It's not that we don't know you."
"I don't run a tab on myself," he said.
Such requited self-love deserves contempt.
    The view of your own flaws is blurred and dark.
Why, then, look on the foibles of your friends
with an eagle's or a snake's eye? For won't
your friends do just the same for you, and list
your failings carefully?
                              "He's touchy. He
smells like wet straw. His bumpkin haircut makes
us laugh; his toga's never met an iron;
his shoes are too big for his feet." But he's
also a good man. But he's your friend. But
he has talents hidden by his rumpled frame.
Ask yourself if nature or your own bad
habits haven't sown in you the seeds of folly:
weeds that you neglect you'll have to burn out
later.
    The lover can't see his lady's
flaws; instead he finds them charming and calls
a wen a beauty mark. We should conduct

our friendships the same way and find a name
other than "error" for this kind practice.
We should treat a friend the way a father
does his child, and not catalog his flaws.
If the son squints, the father calls him Wink.
If he's a runt, like Sisyphus, the name
for him is Chick. He's bow-legged? Call him
Tex. If he wobbles on his pins, call him
Sailor. Is a friend cheap? Let's say thrifty.
Loud and flamboyant? Eager to please sounds
better. Dour and tactless? Frank and fearless.
He's got a temper like a crow's? Let's call him
passionate. This way friends get made and kept,
instead of turning virtues upside down
and scouring a clean vessel with dirt.
Do we know someone modest and truthful?
We call him dull, or bland. How about one
who plays his cards close to his chest and won't
expose himself to malice, since we live
in a world where slander and envy thrive?
We call him insincere, far too crafty.
There's such a thing as too much bumptious
candor (as I've given you, Maecenas,
occasion to think), when someone disrupts
another's time to read or to reflect
merely to chatter. But should we say of
such a man that he has no social
skill at all? These legislations we so
love to make end up punishing ourselves

14

for we're all flawed: the best of us only
bears the least load. A good friend must be fair
and weigh my failings against my virtues
to see which are the more (virtues, prevail!).
For I'll weigh him on the same scale. I'll not
deride his warts; he'll not make fun of mine.
If you want tolerance, you'd best offer
some in trade.
                    Because anger and other
flaws inherent to us can't be rooted
out, why shouldn't we use reason to weigh
the proper punishments for such failings?
Suppose a slave were bid to clear the table
and tasted bits of the half-eaten fish
and its tepid sauce, and so his owner
had him crucified. The owner, sane men
would say, was madder than crazed Labeo,
famous for his draconian sentences.
Here's something even stupider. A friend
has done you some small wrong. You'll seem a fool
if you don't pardon him, but you rage on
and shun him, even as Ruso's debtor
shuns Ruso because the poor wretch can't raise
interest or principal. The due date
looms and like a prisoner of war he'll have
to show his throat and hope his captor won't
read to him his captor's complete works.
What if my friend, one drunken night, leaks pee
onto the couch, or breaks by slurred mistake

a valuable bowl? Suppose he sneaks
hungrily a chicken breast from my
side of the platter. Is he still my friend?
Suppose he stole something, or that he gave
and then betrayed his word, or that he made
bond and then skipped town. If you think all crimes
are equally vile—or have I got your
Stoic doctrine wrong?—you'll have a hard time
with a mirror. Our feelings and customs,
both, rebel against such a silly
doctrine, as does practicality itself,
the mother of justice and right thinking.
      When the first creatures crawled, mute and lumpy,
across the earth, they battled for acorns
and caves with their nails and fists, then with clubs,
and then with better and better weapons
their needs forged, until they found nouns and verbs
to shape their cries and longings, and their world.
They warred less often and they built cities,
and made laws against theft and violence.
And against adultery: long before
Helen's, a cunt started many a war,
though we've no record of the many dead
who took, as beasts do, some female they liked,
only to be slaughtered for it by some
stronger male, the bull of the herd. Law starts
with fear, you've but to think on history
to realize. Nature that knows pleasure
from pain, and danger from desire, can't tell

right from wrong. No more can reason tell us
that it's equally grave to plunder young
cabbages from a neighbor's garden as to
steal religious relics by night. Let's treat
each crime according to the harm it brings,
lest we scourge one who needs but to be whipped.
I don't fear that you'll spank a man who should
be beaten, not since you won't distinguish
between shoplifting and piracy, not
since you'd prune all criminals with the same
huge scythe, if men would only make you king.

    Let's see, the truly wise man is perfect,
right, according to you Stoics? Therefore
he's rich, a skilled cobbler, handsome, a king,
and since you talk as if you're all these things
and yet complain that you're not king, I don't
quite understand. "You twist my words against
me," you complain. "The wise man need never
make shoes for himself to be the finest
cobbler." How's that? "Suppose Hermogenes
is mute when you see him; still he's a great
singer. Alfenus long ago closed up
his shop but he's still a master barber.
Thus the wise man is best at any craft
and that's why he's king." "Spry urchins tug
your bears, Your Majesty; unless you fend
them with your staff, you'll be suffocated,
sputtering and apoplectic, Great Sire,
by your subjects. The reason why you trudge

to the penny baths with a retinue
made up only of that dolt Crispinus
must be, Rex, that it's lonely at the top.
Meanwhile my pals will forgive me if I,
your humble and obedient subject,
screw up, and I'll tender the same mercy
to them, and we'll live not at all like kings,
unless the gods hate us, but like people.

I, iv.

EUPOLIS, Cratinus and Aristophanes
(and the other old poets who first wrote
comedies) freely shamed thieves, skirt-dandlers,
throat-slitters and anyone else famous
for the wrong reasons: they put them on stage.
Lucilius is their true apprentice.
His meters (he's Roman; they're Greek) are new:
he's witty and quick to sniff folly,
but he wrote exceedingly ramshackle.
He'd dictate two hundred lines an hour
with one lobe tied behind his brain. Much mud
needs to be sieved from such floods. He never
learned, that profligate wordslinger, the art
of writing stingily, using only
what's exact and compressed: quantity means
nothing. Crispinus might challenge me,
at long odds, thus: "Let's each take his tablets,
set a time and a place, pick some judges,
and see who writes the most." I thank the gods
for making me slow, timid, and taciturn.
Go ahead, fill yourself like a bellows
and then puff until the fire melts iron,
since that's your way.
                    Think of blithe Fannius,

who offers his books and portrait without
anyone asking. My work goes unread, nor
will I recite it in public: folks don't like
what I write, and why should they, since many
embody the follies I laugh at. Pick
from them at random, chances are good
you've chosen someone wretched with avarice
or ambition. This one pursues the wives
of others; that one slavers for boys. One
lusts for silver, another for bronze. Here's one
who trades from dawn's domains to dusk's gray ports,
swirled on by his greed like dust by a storm,
fearful to lose what he has and fearful
not to swell it by day's end. These people
hate poetry, and the poet: "That bull
has dried blood on his horns. Keep well away.
He'd gore any friend for a laugh, and what
he scrawls anyone can read, even slaves
and old women scuffling home from the public
bakery or from the city water tanks."
    Here's my brief rebuttal. First, I don't call
myself a poet: to put words in meter
is least of all that a true poet does.
My stuff's not poetry; it's inky talk
at best. Eloquence and a noble heart
and being singed by starlight make a poet.
No wonder some have asked if comedy
is poetry or not; it's metrical prose,
really—like speech in its diction, without

the fire or grandeur of inspiration.
"How about this for fire?" you ask. "A father
rages because his son squanders money
on a tart, rejects a wife with a huge
dowry, and lurches drunkenly through town
before dusk." But Pomponius would hear
just such a speech from his father if they
were live people and not stock characters.
It's not enough to write what any wrath-
fueled father might bellow. Take what I write,
or what Lucilius wrote, and muss up
the meter, and exchange a line's first word
for the last, and vice versa. Now sabotage
in the same way
                    "When vile Discord
smashed open the iron gates of war."
From *those* shards a poem could be recognized.
    Enough on this topic; another time
we'll ask if verse like this is poetry
or not. Just now I want to ask you what
you've got against it. Canny Sulcius
and Caprius (informers?) skulk about
crinkling paper, their voices hoarse. Thieves keep clear
of both, but a man with clean hands scorns them.
Just because you resemble Caelius
and Birrius, the robbers, doesn't mean
I'll play Caprius or Sulcius. No
need to fear me. No bookstall sells my poems,
no posted notice praises them, no throng

dusts my little books with fingerprints, not
one blob of Hermogenes' sweat mars them.
Oh, if my friends insist, then I'll recite,
but neither anywhere nor anytime.
Some poets read in the Forum and some
in the baths, whose vaults lend their voices
resonance. They're so pleased to recite they
don't ask if the time or poem is right.

    "You like to cause pain," you say, "that's your goal."
What brickbat is this? None who knows me could
say so. The man who sneers behind a friend's
back, or who won't defend that friend against
the slurs of others, or who'd trade his own
dignity for a spatter of guffaws
and reputation as a wit—his heart's
been charred beyond repair. Beware of him,
my fellow Roman. Often at dinner
the three couches are crammed full, four diners
on each, and one guest sprays the assembly
with insults, excluding the host, of course,
who provides the water. Later, when he's had
enough wine, the host gets spattered, as well,
for Liber, that truthful god and partner
to Bacchus, unlocks the heart's secrets.
You think this guy's the life of the party,
you, who hate the black-hearted. Because I
wrote that "Rufillus smells like a perfume
stall, and Gargonius like a goat,"
do you think me a mean, spiteful black-heart?

If someone joked in your presence about
Pettillius's thefts, you'd defend him,
after your fashion. "He's been my friend
from boyhood; he's done me many good turns;
I'm relieved he's out of danger and not
exiled. And wasn't his acquittal
a miracle?" Now that's squid ink, blacker
than any heart you loathe. There's none of that
on my pages because my heart is free
from it when I sit down to write. If I
can promise anything, I promise that.

    Maybe I use words freely and poke fun
too readily, but you could grant me both
your tolerance and my right. The best
of fathers taught me with fables what I
should shun. His lesson on money
was that I should count it again and find
it enough, for "young Albius is broke
and Baius a few feet from the street:
they spent more than they had from their fond dads."
I had a hot eye for a lurid girl?
"Don't let them compare you to Scetanus."
I grew an urge for someone else's wife?
"You want Trebonius's reputation?
Philosophers will tell you this or that,
and yea or nay, and give you reasons, too.
But I'm content with the rules our fathers left
us, and if, I can keep your name and health
from harm, so long as you need tending.

When your mind and body are both grown strong,
you'll swim without a life jacket." With talk
like that he kept my boyhood on straight course.
Always he used examples. "Do as that
one does," he'd say, pointing to one chosen
for the praetor's jury list; or, should he
hope to defer me from some folly, "Just think
what a storm of stern gossip ensnarled So-
and-So. Would you call that down on yourself?
When a glutton's sick, a neighbor's death seems
a personal warning, and causes reform.
Likewise the youthful mind can be quickly
focused by another's shame.

                              Thanks to training
like this I've shunned the erosive vices,
though I've got mild ones even you, I trust,
would forgive. Some of these sharp time will plow
under. Words from a friend, or from myself,
may lessen some, for when I seem to be
just lazing around, or out for a walk,
I'm on my case. "I know how this one goes."
"The better choice is clear." "This move will please
my pals." "So-and-So made a flagrant ass
of himself that way; could I too ever
be so stupid?" What if my lips are sealed?
It doesn't mean I don't talk to myself.
And then in my spare time I write things down—
one of the milder vices I spoke of.

You'd better not condemn it, lest a swarm
of my fellow poets thicken on you,
and, like the Jews, insist that you join us.

I, v.

JUST PAST Rome's thick shadow I and my friend
Heliodorus, the smartest of all Greeks
and our best rhetorician, spent the night
in a small Arician inn, then next day
idled through the Appian market,
clogged by sailors and greedy bartenders.
Full speed ahead and tunnel vision,
you can make it through there in a day,
but we took two. When not in Rome, why not
do as non-Romans do? The vile water
there slimed over like a foul pond in my
stomach, and the unqueasy dined downstairs.
    The night had wrapped its robe around the earth
and sown the sky with stars. Slaves cursed boatmen
and boatmen snarled at slaves: "Over here, dolt."
"You're loading too damn much." "Enough, enough!"
To collect fares and get the mule harnassed
takes an hour. Gnats bite, frogs croak, none sleeps.
Marinated in green wine, the boatman sings
songs of the woman he left behind. Some sad
passenger sings harmony for a while,
then falls asleep. The boatman knots the mule's
reins to a rock: the mule can graze and he
can sleep. It's dawn when we learn we've not budged,

and then some hot-head flails boatman and mule
awake with a willow switch, and at long
last we're launched.
                        And thus it's nearly ten
a.m. when we wash our faces and hands,
Feronia, in your welcome waters.
Breakfast next, and then we clamber three miles
up to Anxur, gleaming on its rocky
perch. Here we'd meet Maecenas and power-
ful Cocceius, men skilled in state affairs
and at soothing disputes between friends.
Here I daub my aching eyes with black salve.
And then Maecenas and Cocceius come through
the door with Fonteius Capito, that paragon
and best friend to Antony.
                        Fundi we gladly
left in the pompous care of Aufidius Luscus,
an ex-scribe tricked out with a bordered toga,
a broad-striped tunic, and pans of coals for burning
incense when dignitaries visit. Next we collapse
in the Mamurras' city, Fontiae; Murena
gives shelter and Capito food. The next day:
more friends! Plotius, Varius and Virgil
meet us at Sinuessa. No better men have walked
the earth, nor none whom I've loved more. What jokes,
what hugs we exchange! What pleasure equals friendship's?
I've thought, and thought at my smartest, and don't know.
    Near the Campanian bridge a small house
for travellers on government errands

shelters us, and the officers there fed
and supplied us. Next, at Capua, our staunch mules
shed their burdens early. Maecenas goes off
to play ball, but Virgil and I snooze, for ball⁄
tossing ravels the red⁄eyed and queasy.
Next we stay at Cocceius's lush villa,
which overlooks the inns of Caudium.

   Now, my muse, help me recall the battle
between mouthy Sarmentus and Messius
Gamecock, and help me limn the lineage
of each fierce foe. Messius was an Oscan
of good family for an Oscan; the widow
who freed Sarmentus was still alive. But enough
ancestry: on to the fight. Sarmentus
landed the first blow. "You're a stallion."
We laugh. "You better believe it," says Messius,
tossing his head. "Too bad you had the horn
cut from your forehead," Sarmentus jeers;
"now you're but three⁄quarters fierce and ugly."
Sarmentus spews jibes about warts and ugly faces,
and urges Messius to dance as the Cyclops:
he'd need neither a mask nor a costume.
Messius had his comebacks ready.
Had Sarmentus made a votive gift of his
chain to the Lares? Though now a freedman
and a clerk to boot, didn't he still belong
to his mistress? And why had Sarmentus
thought to flee, since a pound of meal, a quarter
of a slave's ration, could feed one so scrawny

and slight. A dinner like that you don't rush,
but let dawdle along.
                              Next we go straight
to Beneventum, where our dithering host
almost burst into flame while turning scrawny thrushes.
Like a scout, a flame slithered from the stove
and shinnied to the ceiling. Famished guests
and frightened slaves rescue the dinner and
all scurry to stifle the flames.
                              From here
Apulia reveals to me her familiar hills, those
the sirocco parches, and over which we'd not
have clambered if a villa near Trevicum
hadn't taken us in and then gassed us with tear-
inducing smoke caused by green wood, leaves
and all, sputtering in the stove. And that night
I lie in wait till midnight, an amorous moron,
for a girl who forgets her glib promise.
Then sleep swirls me away, still smoldering, and so
in dreams I spatter my bedclothes and belly.
    Next we're whisked twenty-four miles by carriages
to a little town I shan't name in verse, it scans
so poorly, though you'll know it when I tell you
that water has to be bought there, and that their bread
is by so far the best that wise travellers take
some for the trip's next stage. For at Canisium,
founded by brave Diomedes long ago, bread
is gritty and there's no water there, either.
Here Varius bids good-bye and his friends weep.

From there we continue to Rubi, arriving
tired from a long slog through mud and rain.
Next the weather was better but the road worse
all the way to the walls of Bari, a fishing town.
Then Gnatia, built without blessing from water-
nymphs, provided us with laughter, at least:
there we were solemnly told that incense
melts without fire on the temple steps.
Apella, the Jew, may believe this, but not I,
who have "learned that the gods lead a calm life,"
and that if Nature should produce a miracle
the gods haven't broken their peace to cause it.
At Brindisi ends a long trip and long story.

I, vi.

OF ALL THE LYDIANS who settled Tuscany,
Maecenas, none has a nobler lineage than you,
whose grandfathers on both sides commanded
great legions. Yet you don't sniff at men
like me, a freedman's son—no pedigree.
　　You ask what difference it might make who
a man's parents are, so long as he's freeborn?
Even before Tullius, son of a slave, became king,
many men of anonymous parents
lived steadfastly and rose to high office,
whereas Laevinus, descended from the same
Valerius who drove Tarquin the Proud
from his throne, was never valued more
highly than they, even by the populace
that all too often, as you well know,
raises worthless louts to office, and gets
dazzled by fame and titles and lineage.
So how should those of us behave who live
apart from all this elbow⸗clanging?
　　Of course the public would rather give
office to Leavinus than to upstart Decius.
And Appius the Censor would have struck
my name from the senatorial lists:
I'm only a freedman's son. He'd have been right—

I'd have been an ass in a lion's skin.
Vanity drags, chained to her gaudy chariot,
the nameless and the famous equally.
Tillius, what good came to you when your
expulsion from the Senate got reversed?
Envy closed its jaws on your familiar
flesh you might have kept ungnawed and private.
When a man winds the Senatorial
black straps around his calf or puffs his chest
out behind the purple stripe, the world asks,
"Who is this guy? Whose son is he?" Likewise,
if one had Barrus's disease (the fever
to be called handsome everywhere) he'd spur
girls in his swath to fierce comparisons:
what's his face like? His calves, feet, teeth? His hair?
He who hopes to help rule Rome (Italy,
and the empire) and to supervise the temples,
invites from any mouth rude questions:
"Who's your father, and your mother, really?
What makes you, son of one slave or other,
fit to condemn our criminals to death?"
"But," you protest, "my colleague Newman sits
but one row behind me, where my father would
have been assigned." And here's the sneered reply:
"Does that make you a Paulus or a Messala?
As for Newman, we could hear his clarion bray
above the din of two hundred carts and three
funeral corteges all colliding
in the Forum, but loud isn't senatorial."

As for me, "a freedman's son," whom none fails
to call "a freedman's son," the glue of envy makes
that true tag cling well now that I'm your friend,
Maecenas, as it did earlier, when I
served as a tribune in Brutus's army.
But then and now differ. I made a dull
officer, it's true, but you choose your friends
by their merits, not their preens and grandeurs.
I'd not say I'm your friend by luck. Virgil,
the best of men, and then good Varius, spoke
well of me to you. When we met I launched
a few syllables and they sank. I had
no famous father, no Tarentine steeds
to spur through my estate. I was only
who I said I was. You were, as usual, curt.
I left. Then nine months later you called me
back to be among your friends. I'm glad
I pleased you, for you judge a man not by
his father's fame but by his heart and conduct.
    If my flaws are small and few, like moles
on a mostly handsome person, and if none
can justly name me stingy or sleazy,
and if (as I truly think) my life is guiltless
and unstained and my friends love me,
I owe this good luck to my father. For he,
though poor and chained to his tiny farm,
would not send me to Flavius's school
with the huge sons of huge centurions,
slates and satchels slung over their left arms,

33

each carrying his tuition in coins
on the Ides of each month. No, he swept me
off to Rome to study like a knight's son,
or a senator's. If anyone noted my clothes
and slaves he'd have thought them bought
with an ancestral fortune. My father himself
stayed with me and led me, himself, among
my teachers. Need I say more? He kept me
chaste, a keystone of virtue, free from taint
in deed and reputation, both. He didn't fear
that if I should practice a modest trade—
become an auctioneer, or tax collector,
like himself—he'd be thereby thought a fool.
Nor would I myself have complained.
For all this I owe him praise and thanks.

So long as I am sane I'll not be ashamed
of such a father, nor will I defend myself,
as many do, by whining that it's not my fault
my patents were not free-born and famous.
That's not my style. If it were natural
to live our lives a second time, and for that
revised life to choose the parents our prides
craved, I'd ask for my own again and spurn
those bloated by rank and insignia.
The world would think me mad, but you, I hope,
would understand. I'm not used to the fuss
and strut of rank. First, I'd need more money—
attendants on the road, callers at home,
horses and grooms to feed, wagons to keep

clean and oiled. It seems that overnight
I'd be too rich ever to be alone.
But now a puny mule's enough to get
me to Tarentum, if I like, although
I'll chafe him with my spare weight and sparse gear.
And none would deride me for being cheap,
praetor Tillius, the way you got scorned
for taking on the road to Tivoli only
five slaves, ample wine, and a chamberpot.
Isn't my life far easier than yours?
    I decide to go out? I go alone.
I'll haggle with vendors. I'll even prowl
the Circus Maximus, thronged with swindlers,
and the Forum, after dark. I like to hear
the fortune-tellers work the crowd, then amble home
to leeks and peas and sturdy bread. Three boys
serve my supper. On a white slab of stone
rest two cups and a ladle. Next to them:
a cheap salt-cellar, and a jug and saucer.
Then I sleep, with no foreboding: I won't
be up early to seek out the usurer's stall
in the Forum. I lie abed until ten.
Then maybe a walk, or after reading
or writing something I'll think fondly on
later, when I'm having my rubdown—and not
using oil filched from the lamps, as Natta does.
When I'm weary, and stronger sunlight nudges me
toward the baths, I shun the Campus, its games
of three-cornered catch. After a light lunch,

just enough to keep my belly from growling,
I stay happily around the house.
                                    I live
unburdened by ambition and like it,
and like knowing I live more happily
than if my grandfather and father
and uncles all had been quaestors.

I, vii

HOW THE HALFBREED Persius got revenge
on poisonous, outlawed Rupilius Rex,
every bartender and barber knows.
Persius, a rich man, had lucrative
business in Clazomenae, also
a gnawing lawsuit, Rex v. Persius.
Persius was aggressive, bold, bitter-
tongued: he could leave skilled badmouths like Barrus
or Sisenna in the dust.
                              What about
Rex? No way they'd settle. (Litigation
means the heroes clash hand-to-hand. Think: could
Hector, son of Priam, shrink from wrath-
crazed Achilles, or vice versa, unless
death do them part? How else had they made their
reputations but by such truculence?
If two cowards clash, or some mis-matched pair
like Diomedes and the Lycian
Glaucus, the likely loser shows his throat
and they exchange armor.) Who was praetor
of rich Asia when all this took place,
when our Persius and Rex ran at each
other like two rams or gladiators?
Brutus, that's who. The courtroom was jammed full.

Persius lays out his case; everyone laughs.
He praises Brutus and his entourage.
"The sun of Asia," he calls Brutus, and
his followers he calls "his helpful stars."
But not Rex, of course, whom he called "Dog-star,"
dread omen of drought and blight. On he surged
like some winter torrent through a steep gorge:
no sane man would tote an axe into that.
Against this raging flood of wit our Rex,
never too swift, hurls back churlish abuse
such as the vine-dresser, behind in his
pruning, uses to shout down the passer-by
who taunts him to finish his work by spring.
    But the Greek Persius, drenched though he may
be by Italian vinegar, throws
himself on the mercy of the court: "O
Brutus, by the great gods I pray you: since
regicide has made your family fame,
this Rex should be easy. Cleave but a state-
less head from a body impolitic."

I, viii.

ONCE I WAS a log, a worthless chunk of fig-wood,
but the carpenter, wondering whether to make a chair
or a Priapus, chose that I become a god. Well then,
I'd be a god who fills thieves and birds with terror.
My stern extended right hand signals thieves to stop,
and the red stake that blares forth from my crotch.
As for the birds, a reed set on my head fools them
so they don't land here in the new gardens.
Once, slaves would pay to have their fellows buried
here, tipped from their strait cells into a cheap box.
Paupers, criminals, slaves ended here, and men
like Allswag, the parasite, and Nomentanus, the spendthrift.
Here a pillar claimed a thousand feet of frontage
and three hundred of depth to discard the dead,
and added that the land, unlike what paltry
property such folks left, could pass to no heirs.
Now the place is wholesome, even livable.
You can stroll the sunny Rampart and not look
gloomily out over a scatter of bleaching bones.
The thieves and vermin usual to the place
gave me less worry than the witches who trouble
human souls with their spells and potions:
I couldn't scare them off from scavenging bones

and magic weeds as soon as the wandering moon
lifted her lovely face above the horizon.
  Here I've seen Canidia stalk barefoot, her black robe
hiked up, her hair a fright—she and the ageless
Sagana shrieking. They were paler than mushrooms.
Then they ripped at the ground with their nails,
then shredded a black lamb with their teeth
and poured its blood into a trench for the shades
to drink (that way the shades could briefly speak):
the witches had some questions for the dead.
They had a wax doll and a woolen one, far larger,
like a governess for the small one, and staged
them so that one hovered and one cringed.
One witch invoked Hecate, the other Tisiphone.
Snakes slithered, hell-hounds bayed. The moon hid
her sweet face behind the taller tombs rather than watch.
It's all true. If not, may the crows strafe me with shit,
and may Julius, and Lady Pediatia,
and Voranus, the thief, prime me with urine
and paint me with dung. Do you want every
detail? The shades keened and lamented the while
Sagana queried them. The furtive witches buried
some wolf-whiskers and the fangs of a mottled
snake. The flames leapt when the wax doll burned.
Of course I trembled while they worked, but soon
enough revenge was mine. A fart that starts
deep in fig-heartwood's like a bomb when it blows free.
The hags sprinted for town. Canidia outran

her teeth and Sagana the leaning tower
of her wig. Herbs, charms, potions: litter.
You should have been there. You'd be laughing still.

I, ix.

I WAS AMBLING along the Via Sacra
in my dreamy way, wholly absorbed,
when up comes a man I know but by name,
and seizes my hand. "How do you do, dearest
fellow?" "I'm getting by," I allow, "which
is not bad, these days. I hope you're thriving."
   He still nipped at my heels, so I asked him:
"There's nothing I can do for you, is there?"
"You must know me," he barked; "I'm a scholar."
"The more power to you," I say, and double
my pace, but then stop short, and then whisper
a word in my slave's ear while sweat slalomed
my legs to my ankles. "O Bolanus,"
I thought more than once, "if only I had your
instant temper." Meantime my adhesive
new friend prattled on about the city:
each street gave him fresh chance for praise.

                                        I said
nothing, to which he replied; "You're restless
to be off, I can see, but it's no use.
I'm yours. I'll go wherever you're headed."
   "I'm going to visit someone you don't know,
who's sick in bed, far across the Tiber,
near Caesar's gardens. Don't let yourself get

dragged around like this."

Then he: "I've got
nothing to do. I like to walk. I'm with
you to the end."

You know how a sulky
donkey's ears sag when he gets loaded hard?
I felt like that.

Then he starts wheedling:
"I'm sure you'll like me better than you do
Viscus or Varius. I can write more poems
faster than they. None dances so daintily
as I, and Hermogenes himself would
pay to sing like me."

"No doubt your mother,"
I tried asking him, "or some other close
relative, depends on you?"

"They're all dead,"
he said.

"Those lucky ones have stranded me.
Won't you dispatch me, too, and seal the fate
a Sabine witch, shaking her urn, foretold
for me when I was but a growing boy?

'No poison for this one,
nor an enemy's sword,
nor some fell disease—
I give you my word.
What will stifle his last breath?
A bore will talk him to death.'"

By then (mid-morning) we'd reached the Temple
of Vesta, and the courts opened their cruel doors,
and he had either to appear and face
his plaintiff or forfeit the suit. "Good friend,"
he pleads; "stand by me. Help me out."

                                        "I'm far
too tired, already, to stand and witness
anything, and I'm a bumpkin about law
and I've a date to keep, and you know where."

   "What should I do?" he asked, "Desert my suit
or you?" "Me, me," I cried. "I won't do that,"
he said, and started off as he led
our crazed parade. I fall right into step,
since I can't find a way to stop this man.

      More wheedling now: "Maecenas treats you well?
He's a man with few friends and much good sense,
and he knows how to bear his good fortune.
I'd serve you well—I'm good at minor roles—
if you'd introduce me to the great man.
Nobody would displace you ever."

   "Life in his house," I said, "is straightforward,
free from intrigue. And it doesn't bother
me if someone else has more money, more
learning; there's room for all of us."

                                 "A rare
household, indeed," the pest then says; "I'm not
sure I can believe it."

                        "But it's true all

the same," I tell him.

"That makes me burn more
brightly to get close to this paragon."

"Why don't you hope for it? A man like you
can storm that fort. It's because Maecenas
can be won that he bristles with defenses."

"I'm on the case. I'll bribe his slaves. If I'm
repelled today, I won't give up, I'll wait
for the right time and meet him in the streets
and then escort him home."

Life grants no man a prize
who doesn't strive and strive.

The babbling pest
surges along this way, like a spring stream,
when whom do I meet but Aristius
Fuscus, my good friend, who, as it turned out
knew my new pal well. We stop. "Where are you
going and where are you coming from?" Asked
and answered. I tug on his cloak, I wink,
I mutely plead for him to rescue me.
He likes a joke salted by cruelty, so
pretended not to understand. I fumed.
"I distinctly remember you told me
you had something to tell me in private."

"Of course I did," he said. "Now's not the time.
Today's the thirtieth Sabbath; would you have

me offend the circumcised Jews?" "You know
I have no scruples," I hiss at him.

                              "Yes,"
he says, "I know. But I, mild conformist
that I am, have a few I still observe,
and so we'll talk another day."

                              What had
I done to be shone on by a black sun?
Fuscus had fled. The knife was at my throat.
    But then the plaintiff foamed up to the pest:
"Don't budge, you wretch!" Next the plaintiff asks me
if I'll attest that the pest is indeed
the defendant, and gleefully I will,
and so signify by tilting my head
so that the plaintiff can touch my eartip.
Thus the pest gets dragged off to court,
and babble ensues, and milling about,
and thus I am rescued by Apollo.

I, x.

IT'S TRUE I said that Lucilius's poems
limp on unsteady feet. Is there a fan
of Lucilius so blindly adoring
that he'd deny it? Yet on the same page
I praise Lucilius for rubbing salt
in the city's wounds.
                    To laud him for that
doesn't praise him for everything.
On such terms I'd have to call Laberius's
stinging low-life skits great poetry.
To wring a laugh from your audience
isn't enough, though it's no small feat.
You've got to be terse, so that your thought
escapes the snare of being said so well
and thoroughly it crams your readers' ears.
You need a style both grave and light. The wise
poet or orator sometimes employs his
power by restraining it. Jokes can slice
knots that blunt earnest attack, as they who
wrote the great Attic comedies knew well.
We should emulate them, whom Hermogenes
has never read, nor that monkey who
imitates Calvus and Catullus.
                              "But

don't you admire the way Lucilius
braided Latin and Greek rhetorics?"
you ask,

and No, I don't; can it be hard
to do what Pitholean of Rhodes did
naturally?

"But a blend of both tongues
surely preserves the best of each, like
mixing Falernian wine with Chian."

I ask you then, do you offer this rule
only for writing poetry, or would
you, defending Petillius against
harsh charges of embezzlement, deploy
your knowledge of the legal Greek you know
Roman judges despise? You'd not refer
to the fatherland and mother tongue while
your opponents wrote their briefs in Latin?
You'd jumble your hometown patois with what-
ever your foreign neighbors speak?

Listen,
I too, Italian-born, long ago wrote
in Greek. But after midnight, when our dreams
are true, a deified Romulus
chastised me: "The Greeks are rich in poets.
Why then haul kindling to the forest?"

So while the Grandiose Bard of the Alps
slays Memnon and fouls the head of the Rhine
with mud, I scribble these playful trifles—
not to be judged in poetry contests,

nor to be trotted out again and again
on stage.
        Fundanius, you're the only
poet alive who charms us with frothy
comedies in which Davus and his smart
mistress bamboozle Chremes one more time.
In iambic trimeter Pollio
sings the exploits of kings. High-spirited
Varius makes the best epics. The muses
of rural life have given to Virgil
sweetness and a light touch. Then there's satire.
Varro Atacinus tried it and failed,
as did others. I do better than they,
though not so well as Lucilius,
who invented satire and who justly
wears its crown.
        But I did say that his stream
runs muddy and needed better straining.
You're a scholar, tell me, is there no slack
line in Homer? Relaxed Lucilius
found nothing to change in Accius's
tragedies? Didn't he laugh at silly
passages in Ennius, though he claimed
himself no better than what he criticized?
Why shouldn't we, reading Lucilius,
ask if it was his temperament or
his coarse subject matter that made his poems
run bumpily, as if their work were but
to mold each line into hexameters

and thus two hundred lines could be got
down before dinner, and the same number
after? The Tuscan Cassius could write
that way, like a river in flood. They say
his collected works and bookcases
together made a fine funeral pyre.

I grant that Lucilius was witty,
not pretentious, and more skillful than you'd
expect from one inventing a new kind
of poem the Greeks never thought of. He wrote
far better than the others of his time.
But if he lived today he'd have to prune
and slash and amputate from what he'd done,
and when he started on new work, to scratch
his copious head bald, and gnaw his nails.

Use both ends of the pencil if you hope
to write what gets read twice. Don't hope to please
the many who buy books; instead treasure
the few who read. Or are you mad enough
to hope your poems get memorized by rote,
though not by heart, in every school? Not I.
Remember the actress Arbuscula?
Booed by the senators and rabble both,
she spat: "It's enough that the knights applaud."

Why let that louse Pantilius, or that
back-biter, Demetrius, annoy me,
or vacuous Fannius, who muddies
my name at Tigellius's table?
Here are those whose respect I hope to have:

Plotius and Varius, Maecenas
and Virgil, Valgius. And Fuscus
and Octavius, also paragons,
and the brothers Viscus. And I name
you, Pollio, without flattery, and
you, Messalla, and your good brother,
and Bibulus and Servius. Honest
Furnius, you too. More literate men
whom I count friends I could name, too, but poems
ought to be brief. I write for their esteem
and if I've fallen short of that, I've erred.
Let Demetrius, and Tigellius,
too, whimper somewhere else, from the soft chairs
of their lady students, perhaps.
                         Hurry,
lad, and add these lines to my little book.

II, i.

HORACE: Some have complained my satires cut
such gashes I should fear libel suits, yet
others call them bloodless and insist satires
just as good could be cranked out a thousand
a day. Tell me, Trebatius, what should
I do? *Trebatius:* Take a break. *Horace:*
You mean write nothing at all? *Trebatius:* Just so.
Horace: Damn me if you're not right, but what then
will I do when I can't sleep? *Trebatius:* Slather
yourself with oil and swim the Tiber back
and forth three times; then, after sunset
marinate yourself in wine. If you must
scribble, try some praise for our unvanquished
Caesar and blush on your way to the bank.
Horace: You're right, best of fathers, but I've not
got the skills I'd need to depict lances
bristling, dying Gauls with broken spears,
a skewered Parthian sliding slackly
from his horse. *Trebatius:* Then why not praise Caesar
for his just rule? Canny Lucilius
did that for Scipio. *Horace:* I'm ready
for that good luck when it's ready for me.
A Flaccus who hopes to pour a few words
in Caesar's ears needs to know when to tilt

his wrist. Curry that horse clumsily
and you'll feel a fusillade of hooves.
Trebatius: this is a better plan than writing
"Allswag, the parasite, and that spendthrift Nomentanus."
A line like that makes anyone think he
could be next, and though unscarred, he fears you.
Horace: Is it my fault that Milonius,
drunk on the fumes of his drunkenness, starts
seeing double and dances with himself?
Castor loves horses; Pollux, born from the same
egg, loves boxing. For every thousand souls
there are a thousand passions. I merely
capture this variety in meter, just
as Lucilius, a better man
than you or I. He confided to his books,
his faithful friends, and told his secrets no⁄
where else, in good times or worse. So his work
lets us view, as on a votive tablet,
the old poet's whole life. I follow his good
example. Whether I'm Apulian
or Lucanian, I don't know; settlers
in Venusia plowed close to borders
of both lands. Those settlers were sent to fill
the space the Samnites had been driven from,
or so the story goes, with this in mind:
to block a free path to Rome if either
the Lucanians or Apulians,
pugnacious races both, should threaten war.
But I'd not thrust my pen at anyone

who'd not provoked me. It's a defensive
weapon, like a sheathed sword. Why would I draw
it when I'm safe from thieves? O Jupiter,
Father and King, may my sword rust away
and no one harm me. Peace and quiet,
that's my ticket. "Hands off" is my motto:
anybody gives me any trouble, he'll be
swiftly famous for his pain and snuffling.
If you irk Cervius he'll yank you into court.
Canidia has poison concocted
by Albucius. If Terrius is judge
when you're in court, expect a savage fine.
We all have ways to ward off enemies,
by courtesy of Nature. Therefore wolves
fight with fangs and bulls with horns. Instinct taught
them how. Suppose prodigal Scaeva has
a long-lived mother. His pious hand
will not strike her. This isn't strange. A wolf
won't kick you, nor a bull bite. Some hemlock
in a honeysop will ease the old crone
into final sleep. Here's what I think: if long
age awaits me or death stretches out
its sable wings just now, rich or poor,
in Rome or in exile, whatever comes,
I can't not write. *Trebatius:* I fear a brief life
for you, young man. Some high-placed friends
of ours could chill you with a killing frost.
Horace: When Lucilius, first to compose
satires like this, peeled back the gleaming pelts

of some who strutted grandiosely
to show what festered underneath,
was Laelius offended, or Scipio,
who made a name for himself at Carthage?
Were they annoyed that Metellus got stung
and Lupus avalanched by apt satires?
Lucilius lampooned alike leaders
and common folk, tribe by tribe, favoring
only virtue and virtue's few friends.
Indeed, when valiant Scipio and wise,
kindly Laelius withdrew from public
matters, they took Lucilius along
and all three chortled while the cabbage boiled.
Lagging after Lucilius in rank
and wit, as I do, I've nonetheless lived
with the powerful, as Envy won't forget.
She'll hope to sink her fangs in something
soft when she strikes me, but she'll blunt them on
solid stuff. Learned Trebatius,
perhaps you disagree? *Trebatius:* Not at all.
But be careful and don't forget the law:
a man who writes scurrilous verse about
another can be called to account in court.
Horace: Scurrilous verse? Sure. But suppose
they're true, and good, and Caesar approves them?
Suppose the honest man who wrote such poems
pleads truth as his defense against libel?
Trebatius: The charge will get tossed out of court
with a snicker, and you'll laugh your way home.

II, ii.

FRIENDS, let's live and eat plainly. My neighbor
Ofellus says so; I'm not citing myself.
His school of thought? He's got his faculties.
They tell him not to decide such questions
when the table gleams with splendors that glaze
the eye and distract judgement. Now, before
we dine, let's talk the matter out. "How's that?"
I'll tell you, if I can. Would you expect
a bribed judge to weigh the truth exactly?
First, work up a sweat hunting a rabbit
or trying to break a horse. Or if our
Roman army sports seem crude compared
to Greek games, play catch, fire the ball harder
and harder so fun disguises hard work
or slice a discus through the pliant air
if that's your pleasure. But get lathered up
and undainty, get parched and get famished,
and then sneer if you can at plain food, spurn
any honey not from Hymettus, or
wine that's not Falernian. The cook's out
for the night, the winter-darkened sea hoards
all its fish. Won't bread and salt by themselves
soothe your snarling belly? Why shouldn't they?
You're the source of your pleasure, not tidbits.

So trade your sweat for sauce. If you're bloated
and blanched from sopping up one best dish
after another, will oysters be your
balm, or trout, or one more imported grouse?
Try as I might, I'll not uproot your bent
for luxury. If a peacock gets served,
you'll forget how good the homely chicken
tastes. You love what doesn't matter: peacock
is scarce, expensive, and spreads its lurid
tail fetchingly. So what? Are the feathers
edible? How pretty does it look cooked?
Both birds taste fine, but you choose between them
by glamor. OK. But how can you tell
if this gasping pike was lured from the sea
or the Tiber, near that river's Tuscan
source or in the swirling currents just off
the *Insula Tiberina*? You fop,
you laud a three-pound mullet, which you'll need
to cut into chic, small portions. Again
you've gone for gaud. Why spurn a big, long pike?
Because nature made the pike large but wrought
the mullet daintily. The way you scorn
common food, you must have forgot hunger.
"Oh, how I love the sight of a vast fish
on a vast dish," cries some tubby glutton
as greedy as a Harpy. May the hot
south wind blow and taint all his condiments.
Already the fresh boar and turbot he
wolfed down spoil in his overcargoed gorge—

queasily cloyed, in need of radishes
and pickles. You still find poor people's food
at royal feasts: cheap eggs and black olives
have good uses. It hasn't been so long
since Gallonius, the auctioneer, served
a sturgeon and earned everyone's contempt.
Why? Did the sea house fewer turbots then?
The turbot was safe, and the stork on its nest,
until our praetor made eating a stork
stylish. Suppose some trend-setter proclaimed
roasted gulls the most elegant new food?
Our fad-fueled youth would flock to gnaw on them.
Ofellus advocates not a stingy
life, but a simple one; there's no merit
in shunning one flaw only to embrace
its opposite. Wretched Avidienus,
aka "Dog," eats his olives five years
old with dogwood berries, and hoards his wine
until it's turned. His oil you couldn't bear
the smell of, though he will carefully mist
the salad with it from a two-pound horn,
dressed in his festive whites for a wedding
or birthday meal. His vinegar he pours
with a free hand. How should a wise man eat,
like Gallonius? Avidienus?
A wolf on one flank, a dog on the other,
as the proverb has it. A wise man shuns
stinginess and luxuries alike.
He won't harangue his slaves while he's planning

dinner, like old Albucius; nor will
he offer his guests greasy water, like
Naevius. Both of them lacked good sense.
Think what blessings a simple life offers.
Good health, best of all. Think what a jumble
of foods does to the stomach, and recall
how well plain, old-fashioned fare treated you.
But if you mix boiled and roast meats, or shell-
fish and thrushes, sweet juices turn sour
and insurrection roils the belly.
Notice how pale the diners are, rising from
one of those many-dished, jigsaw puzzle
dinners? Worse yet, a body still clogged
by yesterday's surfeit drags the mind down
with it: a shard of the divine spirit
gets thus entombed in mud. Another man
eats a light supper and drifts easily
to sleep and wakes freshly to his day's work.
Now and then when the turning year brings him
a holiday, or when he's wan from overwork,
or as he ages and pampers himself a bit,
then he can eat more festively.
But you, you spendthrift, what foods will comfort
you against illness and old age limping
towards you, since you've stuffed your mouth with all
and sundry in your hot and able youth?
Our fathers hung a boar till it was "high,"
not because they lacked noses, but because
the boar might better feed a late-coming

guest than the greedy host when it was fresh.
Oh that I'd been born among such heroes.
You like to be well spoken of. Music
itself is no more welcome at the ear.
Huge turbots and flamboyant dishes
mound up both scandal and expense. Then there's
your stern uncle, angry neighbors and self-
loathing—you'd hang yourself except you can't
afford a rope. "You might scold Trausius
in such a tone of voice," you say, "but I'm
richer than any three kings." There's nothing
better you could spend your surplus for?
Why's any good man poor while you're so rich?
The temples of the gods could use repair.
Are you so shameless you'll give nothing
to your country? Fate won't snicker at you
ever, you must think; what good fun you'll provide
your enemies one of these days. Who will
fare better when his luck changes, one who
coddles mind and body with all comforts,
or one who can get by on little and
prepares for change, the way a wise man
keeps his weapons oiled and sharp in peacetime?
Let me give you a handy example.
When I was a boy Ofellus lived as simply
as he does now. In those days the little farm
he lives on still with his sons and cows
was his, but it got confiscated. Now
he's a tenant-farmer there. Here's his story.

"Most working days I'd eat no more than greens
and the end of a smoked ham. But if friends
came whom I'd not seen for a long time, or
a neighbor dropped by when it was too wet
to work, then we'd celebrate. No fish shipped out
from town, but a fine chicken or a goat.
For dessert: nuts, split figs and some raisins
brought down from the rafters. We drank without
protocol or fuss until Ceres, to whom we
prayed (*May you climb high on stalks!*), smoothed with wine
the creases in our brows. Let Fortune rave
and concoct new troubles, we'll still have those
good times in our hearts. Have we suffered,
my sons, or lost heart, since the new landlord
took over? Nobody can own the land.
Nature signs no deeds. He harried us out,
and in his turn, his sloth or ignorance
of legal trickery, or at the last, an heir
will supplant him. Now the land bears the name
of Umbrenus. Once the name was Ofellus.
Still it belongs to none, and uses us
to till it, one by one. Live as brave men,
then, standing chest to chest with changeful fate."

II, iii.

DAMASIPPUS: You might strive to finish
a poem one of these days; instead, you weave
and unweave like Penelope. Three or four
times a year you call for parchment and write
out a finished poem. You're angry to write
so little, yet lavish with wine and sleep.
What gives? You sought refuge here at the farm
for the Saturnalia, stayed sober,
and what have you produced? Speak up. Nothing?
Don't blame your pen. Don't pound the walls, those banes
of gods and poets. You wore all the way
here the face of one who'd work mightily
under the carefree comfort of his roof.
You packed Plato and Menander,
and lugged Eupolis and Archilochus
also from Rome, and to what use? No more
satires mean no more enemies? Poor wretch,
they'll drown you in contumely. When Sloth,
that blowsy Siren, sings, you'd better stop
your ears, or cede the good name you once earned.
Horace: May the gods and goddesses grant
you, Damasippus, a barber for your
philosopher's beard. But how do you know
so well? Damasippus: Since I lost all my money

on The Street, I've been a free lance,
minding others' business. I learned antiques,
searching for the bronze bowl in which sly old
Sisyphus washed his feet, finding a flaw
in carving here or a wart in casting
there. I set a price—I'm an expert,
after all, and it was true. A hundred
thousand. Gardens? Fine houses? I knew how
to buy them on the cheap. People called me
"Money's Minion." *Horace:* I know it, and I'm
surprised to find you cured of that disease.
Damasippus: It took a new ailment to free me
from the old one, as when a headache
or stitch in the side migrates to the stomach,
or a waning patient revives and beats
his doctor silly. *Horace:* Spare me from that
and you can do as you like. *Damasippus:* Good friend,
don't delude yourself; you're mad, as are all
fools. So says Stertinius, the Stoic
whose maxims I jotted down the very
day he saved me, encouraged me to grow
my beard, talked me down from the Fabrician
bridge and lured me away from depression.
After I went broke, I wanted to hide my
face and hurl myself into the Tiber,
but he stood at my right hand and warned me:
"Watch out! Don't sell yourself short. There's no shame
if those you fear will think you mad are mad
themselves. Let's ask each other, you and I,

who's mad and who's not? If you're the only
madman on the planet then I'll shut up
and let you fling yourself to a brave death.
Whomever willful folly or ignorance
drives blindly on, the Stoics declare him
insane. This includes whole nations, great kings,
everyone except the wise. Now, here's how
those who call you mad are mad. In a wood,
error diverts men from the strict path, some
left, some right. They're all wrong, each in his
way. Who says he's right is of course wrong—
is he the one you'll let pronounce you wrong?
One kind of fool is so wracked by his fear
he invents a world worth fearing: he sees
flame-spires and rocks rise from what is in fact
a level field, and sees hurtling rivers
divide it. Another kind of fool would
amble through a fire or flood, though his dear
mother, sister, father, wife—his whole clan—
cry out, "Beware the ditch. Beware the boulder."
He'd no more hear them than the drunken
actor Fufius, who couldn't be waked
to say the lines of a character roused
from sleep by the script although twelve hundred
playgoers bellowed out the wake-up line.
Such is the numb world, and I'll tell you why.
Damasippus has gone mad buying old
statues. Is Damassipus's creditor
more sane? Ha! Suppose I give you money

you need never pay back? Are you insane
to take it? Would you be crazier still
to scorn the lucky finds that Mercury
sometimes leads us to? Write ten IOUs
to Nerius. Not enough! Add a thousand
payable to Cicuta, the sharpest
loan shark of them all. Shackle the debtor.
But Proetus will slip away from you.
Drag him to court? He'll laugh as you go broke,
and he becomes a boar, a bird, a stone
or a tree. If a good deal is sane and
a bad deal mad, well then Perellius
has gone around the bend. Didn't he lend you
money you can never pay back?

II, iv.

HORACE: Catius, where are you rushing
and from what? *Catius:* Home to jot down
some notes on the wisdoms I just heard.
Pythagoras, Socrates, and Plato—
they've been surpassed! *Horace:* Forgive me if I've
stopped you at a bad time, but that famous
memory of yours—a work of nature
or of art?—will track down all stray details.
Catius: It won't be easy. It's subtle stuff
and woven by a subtle mind. *Horace:* Who
is this wonder? A Roman? A stranger?
Catius: I can't tell you the maestro's name
but I already know his rules by heart.
The more oblong the egg and the less round,
the tastier, whiter and firmer; such
eggs have a male yolk. Cabbages grown on dry
land taste sweeter than the mushy pap raised
nearer to the city; all that water
spoils them. What if a friend drops in on you
at dinner time and the only chicken
you can catch is old, sinewy and tough?
To make it tender, dilute Falernian
with water and drown it in this birdbath.
Don't trust mushrooms not found in the meadows.

For good health all summer, top off your lunch
with black mulberries picked before the sun
is high. Aufidius mixed his honey
with strong Falernian—a disaster!
When the veins are empty, give them nothing
but bland tastes. A mild mead is just the thing
for sluicing out the stomach. If your bowels
get clogged, mussels will blaze a trail,
or any shellfish, or low-growing sorrel
(but only if combined with Coan wine).
Shellfish grow plumper as the new moon swells,
but you've got to know where the best of them
come from. The Lucine mussel is better
than the Baian cockle. The best oysters?
From Circeo. The choicest sea urchins?
From Cape Miseno. Luxurious
Tarentum is proud of its huge scallops.
You can't excel in the art of dining
unless you learn the theory of flavors.
It won't do just to buy inexpensive fish
unless you know which are better with sauce
and which fish, when broiled, will perk a tiring
diner up. The host who wants not to serve
dull meat will seek out an Umbrian boar
fattened on acorns from the holm-oak. Now
there's a porker that will bend the platter,
unlike the insipid Laurentian
boar that forages on marsh grass and reeds.
Deer who've grazed in vineyards are not always

edible. The forelegs of a pregnant
rabbit please the gourmet most. As to fish
and fowl, my palate is the first to judge
exactly their prime age and quality.
Some specialize in finding new sweets,
but everything needs your attention.
Would you have your wines be excellent but
anoint your fish with an improper oil?
Set Massic wine out on a cloudless night—
its coarseness will be soothed, its nerve-jangling
bouquet will dissipate. But you can spoil
the same wine by straining it through linen,
sapping its strength. As for Surrentine wine,
an adept mixes it with the dark lees
of Falernian, then breaks a pigeon's egg
into the mixture. The slowly-sinking
yolk clasps all sediment in its grasp.
You can revive a burning drinker
with fried prawns or fried African snails.
No lettuce. It bobs on the stomach's acids
like a cork. Instead try ham and sausage,
or some hot tidbit from a street vendor.
Learn well the recipe for compound sauce.
The base is sweet olive oil. Mix it with
thick wine and brine in which fine Byzantine
fish have been packed. Mix with chopped herbs and boil.
Sprinkle with Corycian saffron, let
stand, then add some juice squeezed oh so gently
from the very best Vanafran olives.

Apples from Tibur look tastier than
those from Picenum, but they're not. Put up
Venuculan grapes, but smoke Alban grapes
until they're raisins. These last I was first
to serve with apples, as I was to serve
caviar in wine lees, or to sift black salt
and white pepper each mounded on its plate.
It's a crime to spend a small fortune
at the fish market and cramp the finny
giants on a narrow platter. Suppose
a slave has dandled the drinking cup
with hands greasy from filched snacks, or there's mold
on your best antique bowl? Wouldn't that turn
your stomach? Brooms, dishcloths, sawdust—how much
does it cost to fend off scandal? Would you
sweep mosaic pavements with a dirty
broom of palm-leaves, or toss grimy covers
on good upholstery? The less it costs to do
things right, the more's the blame if they're undone.
These are not cares only the rich can take.
Horace: Catius, you scholar, swear by the gods
and in the name of friendship that you'll take
me to the next lecture you attend.
Second-hand is second best; I want to see
this wizard for myself, as you have done.
I want to visit this pilgrim's fountain
and drink the precepts for a happy life.

II, v.

ULYSSES: A last question, Tiresias:
how can I recover my lost fortune?
What's so funny? *Tiresias:* Well,
I see that canny Ulysses won't be
content only to sail back to Ithaca
and gaze fondly on his household gods.
Ulysses: But I'll arrive naked and broke,
as you foretold, my herds and my cellar
ransacked by the suitors. My noble birth
and character count for no more than kelp
unless they're backed by money. *Tiresias:* Because
it's poverty you dread, I'll tell you how you
can grow rich. Suppose you're given a thrush
or other delicacy. Let it fly
where grandeur and old age prop each other
up. Give the rich dodderer your first fruits—
he's venerated more than the *lares,* after all.
Did he perjure himself? Is he low-born?
Has he murdered his brother or escaped
from slavery? No matter. Should he ask
you to walk with him, take the outer side.
Ulysses: What? Give the wall to some lout? At Troy
I fought only against my betters.
Tiresius: Such honor will cement your poverty.

Ulysses: I'll order my brave soul to weather
this assault. I've endured worse in times past.
So, prophet, tell me how I can rake up
mounds of money. *Tiresius:* OK, I'll tell you
one more time. Troll craftily for old men's
wills. The shrewd ones will eat your bait and slip
your hook, but don't give up; fish on through your
frustration. Find a lawsuit underway
in the Forum, for heavy stakes or small,
and befriend whichever party is rich
and childless. No matter if he's dragged into
court a better man on a flimsy cause—
has the better man a son? A wife?
"Quintus," you'll murmur, or "Publius"
(his ears will pivot like a bat's), "justice
makes me your friend. I understand the law's
mazes. I know how to argue a case.
They'll not scorn you nor filch a hazelnut
from you unless they first pluck out my eyes."
Urge him to go home and tend his hide;
you'll conduct his campaign. Then soldier on,
despite the weather, even if "the red-
hot Dogstar cracks mute statues in half," or
(as the bombastic Furius might have
written after lining his stomach with
tripe stew), "Jupiter spatters the frozen
Alps with patchy snow." And then won't someone
lodge a knowing elbow in his pal's rib
and say what a staunch, dedicated friend

you make? And won't new fish circumspectly
swim beneath your boat, considering your bait?
Abject attention to the childless
rich could give your game away, but suppose
some Croesus has a sickly son to rear?
Sufficient smarm could make you second heir.
If the boy dies, you can't help it if you're
lucky. What if your man gives you his will
to read? Decline. Push it away. But steal
a glimpse at line two on the first page
to see if you're sole heir or if you split
the take with others. Some night magistrate
refashioned as a scribe might well outwit
a legacy hunter as Coranus,
playing the role of the crow, outsmarted
Nasica, cast as the fox. *Ulysses:* Are you mad,
or do you spout such murk to make me look
foolish? *Tiresias:* O son of Laertes, my words
will prove true or false, for Apollo gave
me prophetic powers. *Ulysses:* But what does
that story mean? *Tiresias:* In the days when a young
hero, scourge of the Parthians and direct
descendant of Aeneas, shall prevail
on land and sea, avid Coranus will wed
Nasica's daughter. And Nasica owes
Coranus money. Perhaps Nasica
will forgive the debt in his will, or leave
an inheritance? Coranus will give
Nasica his will to read, the latter

will decline time and again, then relent
and read greedily, and find nothing
left to him and his heirs but to complain.
Here's another trick: if some sly woman
or freedman has won some rich dotard's trust,
link arms with them. Praise them and they'll praise
you when they're not there. Not a bad plan, but
it's best to storm the fort yourself. Money-
bags writes poems? Praise them. He likes to lift
skirts? Don't wait to be asked; offer your wife
to the old goat. *Ulysses:* Can she be tempted,
good, pure Penelope whom the suitors could
not turn from her strict path? *Tiresias:* Those Greeks bore
no gifts but came with hands outstretched. They sought
not love but food. Of course your Penelope
was true. But let her glimpse some gold the two
of you could share, and she'll cling to her chance
like a hound to a hide with some nuggets
of fat still on it. I'll tell you something
that happened when I was old. A sly
crone from Thebes mandated in her will
that she be carried to the pyre by her heir
on his bare shoulders, and that her corpse be
well oiled. She could give him the slip at last
who had been too much with her in her life.
You have to be careful. Don't be eager;
don't be diffident. Don't babble too much;
it irks the glum. But still waters don't run.
Act like Davus in the comedy—head bowed,

deferential. Flattery is crucial.
If the wind kicks up, beg him to cover
his dear head. Run interference for him
through a crowd. Tilt your ear when he talks.
You hate how he's a sponge for praise? Lob praise
at him until he throws his arms skyward
in surrender. Fill his ego's balloon
with unctuous breath until it pops. And when
he quits his claim on your long servitude
and care, and, not dreaming, you hear the phrase
"I leave Ulysses a quarter of my
estate," prepare to sow phrases like this:
"My good Dama, gone? How can I bear it?"
Weep some if it won't crumple your straight face.
Suppose plans for the tomb get left to you?
Don't stint. Let his money buy you honor.
Among the other heirs there must be one
older than you, maybe with a bad cough.
Is there some land or a house that fell
to you that he might want? Out of respect,
might you offer it to him for a song?
Enough, Queen Proserpina reels me in.
May you thrive and prosper and live long.

II, vi.

I PRAYED for this: a modest swatch of land
where I could garden, an ever-flowing spring
close by, and a small patch of woods above
the house. The gods gave all I asked and more.
I pray for nothing more, O Mercury, but
that these blessings last my life's full term.
If I haven't cobbled my property
together by a series of gray deals,
neither will I shrink it by squanderings
or neglect. I'm not one to mope: "O if
only I could acquire that neighboring
corner, that mars the shape of my small farm."
Or, "O for the luck of the plowman who unearthed
enough buried treasure to buy the very
land he once had worked for hire, thanks to great
Hercules." I have what I wanted and am
content, and so ask only that my herd
and all else I maintain, except my wits,
grow fat, and that you, steadfast Mercury,
remain my guardian. Now that I've fled
the city to my mountain retreat,
what else should I invoke my prosy muse
to help me praise? There's no social climbing
here, no stifling sirocco to promote brisk

trade for the morticians. Father of Dawn,
or Janus, if you prefer, to whom morning
tasks, by heaven's will, are consecrated,
I start my song with you. The days begin
at a sprint in Rome: you shoo me along
to court to testify for a friend. "Get
cracking or someone will beat you to it."
The north wind harries Rome; the dark stays
longer every day; and I'm out early
nonetheless. What I say in court may well
come back to haunt me. Then I'm on the street,
stepping on some laggard's heel. "You moron,"
he assails me. "Well, it's Horace," he says,
"knocking anyone aside who might slow
his rush to get back to Maecenas's side."
That name is honey to me, I admit
But once I reach the gloomy Esquiline,
the needs of others flood me. "Roscius
will meet you at Libo's Wall tomorrow
morning before seven." "Quintus, the clerks
remind you to go back to the Forum
today for an important guild matter."
"Please have Maecenas set his seal to these
papers." "I'll try," I say. "You can do it
if you want to," I hear next. It's seven
years now, almost eight, since Maecenas made
me his friend for company on trips
and small talk. Such as? "What time is it?" Or,
"Can The Thracian Bantam beat The Hulk?"

Or, "Dress warmly; the cold has filed its teeth."
Chatter you can pour into a leaky ear.
For such intimacy our friend Horace
drew envy. Didn't he and Maecenas
watch the games together; didn't they play
toss on the Campus? "Isn't he the son
of Fortune?" one and all asked. Is there
a rumor on the air? Horace will know
the story from his high-placed pals. "What's up
in the Balkans?" "I don't know," I admit,
and hear a knowing snicker. Let the gods
strike me if I lie. "About those land-grants
Caesar promised his veterans, will they
be on Sicily or on the mainland?"
I don't know, and my interlocutors
treat me like the deep grave of state secrets.
While I waste my days on such piffle,
I pray under my breath: O farm of mine,
when will I see you next? When will I read
the classics, sleep late, laze thoughtfully through
days rinsed free from care? When will I taste beans,
Pythagoras's cousins, and some greens
cooked with bacon? My lar presides over
nights and dinners the gods might envy, when
my friends and I eat well and there's enough
left over for the noisy slaves. Each guest
drinks without protocol or fuss as much
or little as he likes at his own pace.
And then we talk, not about what others

own, or if Lepos is a great dancer
or a bumblefoot, but whether money
or virtue can buy happiness, whether
self-interest or a true heart draws friends,
and what it means to be or to do good.
Now and then my neighbor Cervius
tells us a fable. If one of us should
forget the dreads of wealth, he'd tell this one:
"Once upon a time, a country mouse
welcomed his old pal, a city mouse,
to his sparse hole. It wasn't much. He kept
a rustic larder, but he would open
it wide to guests. How wide? He'd give away
the last chickpea or long oat he'd stored up,
and tote in his teeth a raisin or bacon
scrap to prickle his urban friend's refined
palate. He lay back on his couch of chaff,
eating spelt and darnel, and let his guest
dine on the treats. And then his guest spoke up.
'What pleasures, friend, does this hardscrabble life
provide, perched on the edge of a steep wood?
What about people, and the great city?
Come there with me. We're all slated for death,
whether we be grand or ordinary;
thus we should avidly pursue life's joys
the whole of our short course on earth.' These words
burned in the rustic's heart, and happily
he left his bare home behind. The two mice
set out for the city, planning to wriggle

under the city wall at night. And night
had reached the halfway point of heaven
when they set paw in a rich man's palace,
where crimson cloth gleamed from ivory couches
and leftovers from last night's feast were piled
high in baskets. The city mouse installs
his pal on the plush covers and scurries
about like a deft waiter, serving course
after course and tasting each one first just
like a proper slave. The country mouse
knows how to play the pampered guest
and settles in to enjoy his changed lot.
Suddenly the doors bang open and the mice
tumble from their couches. Fear speeds the pair
the whole length of the room and the house
begins to vibrate with the harsh barking
of tremendous hounds. Then the country
mouse says, 'I don't need any of this, and so
good-bye to it. I long for my safe woods
and bare hole, and a small meal of vetch.'"

II, vii.

DAVUS: I'm only a slave, but I've got ears
you've flooded with nonsense, and thus some things
to say. *Horace:* Davus? *Davus:* A loyal
slave, but not so good that he need die young.
Horace: During Saturnalia you can
say what you will. *Davus:* Some men naturally
love vice. Most of us hope to be good but
sometimes miss that mark. We waver, like
Priscus, who often wore three rings, but now
and again wore none. He changed his stripe by
the hour. He'd follow his whim from mansion
to hovel, the kind a freedman would hope
never to be seen leaving. In Rome he played
a roué, and in Athens a scholar.
Of course Vertumnus, the shape-shifting god
of the changing year, hated Priscus.
By contrast, Volanerius stayed true
to his vice. When the gout he had coming
to him crippled his fingers, he rented
a man by the day to handle the dice
for him. Won't he be better off than one
who strains at his tether, chafing himself?
Horace: Is there a point to this blather? *Davus:*
You're the point. *Horace:* Explain yourself, pondscum.

Davus: You can't speak too fondly of the good
old days but if the great dead men you love
to praise came to invite you back with them,
you'd balk and sulk to stay, either because
you don't mean what you like to say, or because
you won't put up a fight, so your foot's stuck
in the mud while you squirm to pull it out.
In Rome you pine for the country, but once
you're there all your fond talk's of Rome. Are two
faces enough for you? If nobody's
invited you to dinner, you praise simple food.
What freedom you loll in, not going out,
as if some wine with friends were an arrest.
What if Maecenas sends as late as dusk
a dinner invitation? Instant dither:
"Bring lamp-oil instantly! Is no one there?"
You bellow, you berate, you dash away,
and meanwhile your deserted dinner guests
hurl at our back curses I won't quote.
I will tell you how Mulvius complained:
"OK, I'm a slut for food, my nostrils twitch
blocks from a kitchen, I'm lazy and weak
and a feedbag with legs. But since you're no
better, and maybe worse, will you presume
to act superior and throw over
your craven acts a cloak of shapely words?"
You may well be a greater fool even
than I, for whom you paid a bargain price.
Don't scowl at me. Keep your hands and temper

82

to yourself while I tell you what I've learned
from Crispinus's porter. Some one else's
wife enslaves you. Davus? Some whore's got him.
Which crime is more serious? When nature
prods me, a girl lies naked in lamplight
and I prod her, or sweet jockey, she rides
me hard. Then we part. My reputation's
safe. I don't worry who my rivals are.
But you shed your rank to be with your bawd.
No knight's ring, no toga, a hood over
your perfumed hair: a citizen disguised
as a slave may be, in truth, a slave.
You slink into the house, half-lust, half-fear.
What's worse, discovery (the cane, the sword)
or cringing in some cabinet the maid
stuffs you in like laundry, your head between
your shaking knees? Her husband's got the right
to scourge you both, specially you. She's not
disguised herself; you thrust yourself on her;
the poor, dazed creature's been badly misled.
And you're turning like a quail on a spit
your sweetie's husband turns the handle of.
You escaped? Well then, you'll be careful now?
No, you're eager to double your lost bet,
slave who sells himself. What animal would
slither from the trap and then go back?
"I'm no adulterer," you say. OK,
then I'm no thief. I polish your silver
and it stays put. What if I knew I'd not

be caught? The untied horse eats where it will.
Fellow slave, you call yourself my master?
Your friends command you, and your busy life.
You could be made a freedman three or four
times over and not be released from fear.
And think about this: is one who obeys
a slave a sub⁄slave, as the rank⁄happy
love to say, or in fact a fellow slave,
as I am to you? You boss me about
but you've got masters everywhere whose
whims and urges spin you like a top.
Who then is free? The wise man who's master
of himself, who doesn't fear poverty,
prison or death. He's complete in himself
and round, like a stone. He's so slick you can't
get a grip on him, and if you pound him,
you only maim your hand. Are you like this
in any way? Your lover demands money,
bullies you, slams the door in your face, pours
ice water on you, then calls you sweetly
back, and you, milk ox, volunteer your neck
to the yoke. Repeat after me: "I'm free. Free."
You can't. You're learning better to be led,
better thrashed, and better driven where she will.
When you gape at a Parsias—what color,
what tastefully rendered genitals!—
are you better than I standing stock still
before gladiatorial posters—
a few deft strokes of charcoal and red chalk

and my heroes seem to flash their weapons,
to strike, to parry. Is Davus riff-raff
and Horace a dévoté of great art?
Some street snack makes me slaver? What a lout!
You're too refined to inhale rich dinners?
My gut's regular plaint is worse than yours?
Well, I can be flayed, but you're punished, too:
those tastes you've acquired run up quite a tab.
Too many dainties sour the mouth and bloat
the body the bad legs have to heft home.
Think how you'd vilify a slave who stole
a brush to trade for grapes at dusk. Is one
who sells off his estates to entertain
a fussy belly any less a slave?
Also, you can't abide to be alone,
you can't relax, you'd give yourself the slip
if you knew how, and since you don't, you hope
that wine and sleep will stay the black dog
who's been, since you first fed him, your best friend.
Horace: I wish I had a stone. *Davus:* What for?
Horace: Or an arrow would do. *Davus:* The man's
insane, or else a poet. *Horace:* Get your
scurvy ass out of here if you don't want
to be the ninth of nine drudges who tend,
while I write about it, my Sabine farm.

II, viii.

HORACE: How was your grand feast with the rich
Nasidienus? Yesterday I sent
a dinner invitation for you, and
learned that you'd been at the table since noon.
Fundanius: The meal of a lifetime.
Horace: And the first solace for a growling
stomach was?... *Fundanius:* First, wild boar snared during
the gentlest southern breeze, as the dinner's
father reassured us. It came escorted
by savory turnips, greens, radishes—stuff
that jump-starts a stalled palate—carroway,
pickled fish, and wine lees (Coan). When these
were cleared, a servant with his apron tucked
up wiped the maple table with a purple
cloth; another swept up scraps lest they irk
the guests. Then, like some Attic virgin
bearing the emblem of Ceres
in procession came swarthy Hydaspes
with Caecuban wine, and Alcon with some
Chian far too good to salt. "Maecenas,"
said our host, "I've got some Falernian,
or Alban if you'd prefer." *Horace:* Pity
the rich. But tell me, who were your partners
in lush crime? Tell me everything. *Fundanius:*

I sat at the top, Viscus next to me,
and then, I think, Varius. The middle
couch held Maecenas and his retinue,
i.e., Vibidius and Balatro,
two shadows. Nomentanus sat above
our host and Porcius, gobbling tarts whole,
below. Nomentanus was deputed
to point out the wonders we were eating
so we ordinary folk would not think
something special merely weird, like the dish
of flounder livers and turbot livers
that came next. The honey apples took
their red sheen from being picked by waning
moonlight. No doubt Nomentanus could tell
you how that works. Then Vibidius said
to Balatro, "Let's drink him bankrupt
for revenge," and called for larger goblets.
Our host grew pale. He fears hard drinkers
either because wine loosens their tongues or blurs
their palates. The two enthusiasts tilt
whole jugs of wine into vast Allifan
goblets. So did the rest of us except
our host and the two toadies on his couch.
Next came a lamprey splayed on its platter
with shrimp swimming all around it, and with
commentary from the master: "This one
was caught before spawning, which would coarsen
its flesh. The sauce? Oil from Venafrum (first
pressing, of course), roe from the belly

of a Spanish mackerel, five year old
domestic wine added during boiling
(after boiling, Chian is the right choice),
white pepper and vinegar fermented
from a Lesbian wine. I was the first
to boil arugula and elecampane
in the sauce. Curtillis would use sea
urchins, unwashed, as the seas makes the best
pickling compound." Just then a wall-hanging
fell, snapping the fish platter and saucing
the shambled table with more dust than
the north wind blows loose from Campania.
We cringed. What disaster came next? Well, none,
so we relaxed. Our host wept torrents,
as if his son had died. Nomentanus
saved us from who knows what with these words:
"Fortune, most cruel of all the gods, what
would you do for laughs without us humans?"
Behind his napkin Varius snickered.
Then cynical Balatro spoke: "Life works
like this: rewards are small and efforts huge.
Just think, to entertain me royally
you are tortured at every turn.
Will the toast burn? The sauce curdle?
The servants dress properly and prove well-
groomed? Anything could go wrong. The wall-
hanging could tumble, as it did just now;
some oaf could trip and break a serving dish.
But like a general, a host displays

his genius best under disaster."
This swarm makes Nasidienus gush:
"May all the blessings you pray for be yours,
kindest of men, most civil of guests, "
and then he called for his slippers. Whispers
surged swiftly among the assembled. *Horace:*
Better than a night at the theater.
What came next to laugh at? *Fundanius:* Vibidius
asked the servants if the wine-jugs, too,
got broken, since the wine he clamored for
had not arrived. Belatro echoed him.
Anything seemed funny. Nasidienus,
meanwhile, strode in, his shoulders squared; he would
tame chaos with art. His servants lugged in
on a door-sized board a crane's leg salted
and dusted with meal, the liver of a fig-
fed albino goose, and some rabbit legs
(they taste better severed from the loin).
Then blackbirds with charred breasts and rumpless
pigeons. Each dish meant an explanation
of its very essence, and so we fled,
and for revenge we ate no more that day,
as though each dish were broiled by Canidia's
breath, deadlier than any African snake.

Line 5: *Maia, nate:* Son of Maia, Mercury, god of luck and gain.

Line 16: Hercules is god of, among other things, treasure-troves.

Line 25: Janus is invoked as "Father of Dawn" because that's when Horace is writing these lines. His peaceful writing regimen makes a sharp contrast to the blithering pace of Roman life at the same hour.

Line 39: Maecenas, a wealthy Roman, close friend and advisor to Octavian (later Augustus Caesar), gave Horace his "Sabine Farm," the very plot of suburban land this satire describes.

Line 41: The Esquiline was once a cemetery (thus "gloomy") where paupers, criminals, etc. were buried. Maecenas built some splendid gardens there.

Line 43: Libo's Wall: the site of the Roman exchange.

Line 44: The Quintus addressed here is Horace. Horace was formerly a *scriba,* a bureaucrat in the Treasury.

Lines 60–61: "is there/ a rumor on the air?" Maecenas was in charge of Rome during Octavian's absence in 31 BC.

Line 74–75: "beans,/ Pythagoras's cousins…" Pythagoras forbade eating meat because of his doctrine of the transmigration of souls. He also forbade eating beans, and here Horace wryly pretends to think that proscription is for the same reason.

Line 76: "lar": a household god.

Line 80: At fancy Roman banquets elaborate procedures governed drinking and toasts.

Line 100: "Spelt and darnel": the culinary equivalent of millet.

Quintus Horatius Flaccus (65–8BC) published his second book of satires, eight of them, in 30 BC. There's internal evidence in II, vi—a reference to Maecenas's stewardship of Rome during Octavian's travels in 31 BC—that suggests it might have been the last of his satires Horace wrote. II, vi has been the most widely admired of his satires, and, because its fable of the country mouse and the city mouse formed an episode in Disney's "Fantasia," the only one much known outside the precincts of literature.

I've translated all of Horace's satires now; I did this one next to last. Thus a number of decisions that perplexed me when I was translating the first satires I undertook had been made (and remade, when necessary) long before I got to this one.

Because I didn't try to translate a line of Horace with a line of English, my versions would be some lines longer than their Latin originals. In this case the Latin runs 117 lines and my translation uses 131. But Horace wrote in hexameter, and my line is blank verse; if we were counting syllables, my version would be shorter than the original.

I decided to incorporate footnotes into the text of my translations whenever possible. Thus where Horace apostrophizes the "son of Maia," whom Roman readers knew to be Mercury, I finesse the American reader's likely need for a footnote by rendering *Maia natae* as "Mercury."

There are passages where the exact references of the Latin are unlikely to be known to the general reader, but where the context of the poem's development makes it clear what's under discussion. For example, who's "Roscius" in line 42? Obviously enough, someone whom the beleaguered city Horace must meet early in the morning. Who are The Thracian Bantam and The Hulk, in line 53? Probably gladiators. "What's up in the Balkans?" (lines 62–63). It doesn't matter; the point is that Horace is close enough to Maecenas that people are trying to pry inside information from him. It would be pedantic to footnote such passages; their effect is clear enough.

Just as the poem has two mice, it has two Horaces. The country Horace contentedly writes the very poem we read. The city Horace is a frenetic figure, sped up and comic, like a Keystone Cop.

The poem is beautifully structured. It starts on the Sabine Farm (1–28), switches to the city Horace and his urban dither (29–76), returns us to comparative ease and simplicity of the farm (76–110), and then takes the two mice back to the city to be terrified and chastened (110–131).

Each of these sections has a characteristic tone and pace in the Latin, and a good translation must register them in English. The first passage is both thankful and prayerful; the reader must hear Horace's gratitude and contentment. The second passage is crowded and sped up, and then begins to slow its pace (70–76) until, after "bacon" in line 76, we're back on country timing. The fable of the two mice (91–131) starts off at a relaxed and anecdotal pace, but at the point where the mice enter the city (110) the diction grows more literary. "And night/ had reached the half-way point of heaven" (112–113) is meant to suggest a more sophisticated narrator than Horace's neighbor Cervius; a reader who hears the extra loftiness in the language may well suppose that a gentle parody of the descent-into-the-underworld motif is now in progress. The sweetly comic play-acting of the mice serves as a lull, and then the poem speeds to its end and rueful moral.

Horace called these poems *sermonae*, meaning not "sermons" in the modern sense but suggesting a tone—informal, personal, instructive and entertaining. A similar tone in modern writing is more likely to be found in a "personal essay" (cf. "prosy muse" in line 22) than in a satire. E.B. White's essays sound to me more Horatian than most contemporary poetry I can think of.

All translators strive for accuracy, of course, by which we mean fidelity to the text, and to what we can know from it of what the author meant. Horace poses a challenge because he is both a classical author, thus requiring of his translators more than casual knowledge of Roman life and poetry, and a classic, the most quoted author of antiquity. He is alike playful and thoughtful, passionate and ironic, and the poise these balanced attributes create is something to which a translator must also be loyal. Horace didn't sound like a classic to his contemporaries.

There are times when what the translator knows about the cultural background of the originals must serve the freshness and accessibility of the translation and go unnoticed by the reader of the translations. For example, consider this brief passage from another (II, viii) Horace satire.

> *Vibidius dum*
> *querit de pueris num sit quoque fracta lagoena,*
> *quod sibi poscenti non dentur pocula, dumque*
> *ridetur fictis rerum Balatrone secundo,*
> *Nasidiene, redis mutatae frontis, ut arte*
> *emendaturus fortunam.*

A dinner party is underway and fast becoming a disaster. A wall hanging has broken loose and fallen on the pretentious main course. Vibidius and Balatro are raucous guests. Nasidienus, the host, is at first driven from the room by the debacle, then comes back in determination to save the evening. I translate the passage thus:

> Vibidius
> asked the servants if the wine-jugs, too
> were broken, since the wine he clamored for
> had not arrived. Balatro echoed him.
> Anything seemed funny. Nasidienus,
> meantime strode in, his shoulders squared:
> he would tame chaos with art.

The phrase I translated as "with shoulders squared" is *mutatae frontis*, literally "with changed brow" or "forehead."

Here's how three contemporary translators of Horace handle the phrase. First, Smith Palmer Bovie:

"with a brand new look on your face ..."

Jacob Fuchs gives us

"You looked better ..."

And Niall Rudd, the formidable Horace scholar, offers

"Nasidienus re‑enters wearing the face of a man resolved ..."

Rudd comes closest to the sense of the passage, I believe. The brow was in Roman physiognomy the seat of resolve, and the fun of this passage is that our dithering host is about to apply will where only grace will get the job done.

But of course the brow is not the seat of resolve to an American reader, unless he or she has spent a lot of time staring at Roman bust portraiture. When we're about to commit the mess Nasidienus makes, we square our shoulders.

A NOTE OF APPRECIATION

This book would never have come into being without the help of Richard Jackson, who first suggested to William Matthews that he reread the *Satires* with an eye toward a fresh translation. Throughout the years of work, the two of them kept up a lively exchange, with Jackson providing the kind of critical response and personal encouragement that are invaluable to a translator. He was the primary, and often the only, audience during the creation of this work. The estate of William Matthews would like to express its deep appreciation for his generous contribution.